TIME-TRAVELLING TRAIN
ON THE TAMAR VALLEY LINE

Written by
Rachel Gippetti

Illustrated by
Brendan Kearney

It took builders and engineers 50 years to pound out the tracks. Finally, at 8.33 am, one frosty Monday in March 1908, the first train fired up its steam engine at Bere Alston and started off on its journey to Callington. Joyful crowds cheered at each station along the line.

Platform 1
Platform 2
Exit

WANTED
Dr Beeching
REWARD

THE
TAMAR TIMES
1908

OPEN AT LAST!

No more waiting for the tides or struggling for hours on the bumpy roads with a horse and cart — the Plymouth, Devonport and South Western Junction Railway is now open!

TAMAR EXPRESS
753

Today's trip on the Tamar Valley Line won't just show you beautiful views. We'll be going forwards, backwards and hanging over 35 metres in the air! We'll also be meeting some friends of mine as we travel down the line... friends I've known for a very long time...

Brace yourselves as we approach Dockyard Station and the year 1941! Bombs are flying – we must be in the middle of an air raid. Don't worry – we won't stop long.

During the Second World War, troops, weapons, ammunition and other supplies were transported on the railways. Extra carriages were added to the Tamar Valley Line to help the war effort, making the line a target for enemy bombers.

As it was such an important naval base, the Dockyard was a major target too! Unfortunately the rest of Plymouth also paid the price, suffering 59 bombing raids.

THE TAMAR TIMES

1941

Bombs Burst Royals' Hopes

Two days after King George VI and Queen Elizabeth's visit, Plymouth has experienced a brutal wave of bombings that have left homes in ruin and Plymouth citizens dead on the streets.

First *f* Great Western

The city centre was almost completely destroyed and over 1,000 innocent civilians were killed. Devonport was nearly flattened in just two nights of bombing!

Luckily for us, we're just passing through. We'll stop quickly to pick up my friend Bobby, then he can tell you all about life here during the Second World War...

DOCKYARD

WANTED
Dr Beeching

REWARD

Bobby's Story

Since the war started, there's hardly any food. I skip breakfast most mornings. On my way to school I have to step over pieces of shrapnel from exploded bombs - once, a piece cut right through my shoe! When I get to school, instead of exams or normal lessons, we have air-raid drills and learn how to identify warplanes.

At night, when the raids get bad, my mum takes me and my brothers on the train to Cornwall - it's safer there. Sometimes the attacks are so heavy that the trains stop running - we have to go by boat or bus instead. We stayed in Cornwall almost every night last week and slept on the floor of a school. Imagine our horror when we stepped off the train, just last Thursday, to find that our house was a pile of rubble! The Tamar Valley Line had saved our lives.

Bobby

We're just pulling into Bere Ferrers and sliding even further back in time, to 1917! Boarding here is Nathaniel Gately, a soldier who came all the way from New Zealand to fight alongside the British in a different war – the First World War! He seems upset, but who can blame him considering what just happened – a terrible tragedy...

Britain joined the war in 1914, and New Zealand, loyal to Britain, immediately joined in too. During the war, the railways were used to transport soldiers and weapons to the docks and training camps. There was no fighting in Plymouth, but some schools were turned into hospitals, or filled with beds for soldiers to sleep in. Fancy missiles and big bombs hadn't been invented then, but the use of machine guns, poison gas, tanks and even barbed wire made this war one of the deadliest in history!

Nathaniel's Story

It took months at sea to get from New Zealand to Plymouth. After we docked, we got straight onto a crowded train, heading for the army base. We were sick and weak from the long journey. Our backs ached and our stomachs growled. We hadn't eaten in ten hours!

When the train braked suddenly, we thought it was lunchtime and piled out of the carriage – through the wrong door! We fell straight onto the tracks! A whistle sounded and men scrambled to climb up onto the platform. A huge steam train was thundering towards us! It all happened so fast – the brakes shrieked, I dived to the side, pain ripped through my arm... I was lucky; I escaped with my life. Ten of my friends died that day.

Nathaniel

Nowadays, when you pull into Bere Ferrers station you're greeted with a much more pleasant sight: a collection of restored steam carriages, an antique track and a whole train full of photographs and information about the line. But the tragedy has not been forgotten. Just under the station sign, next to a patch of roses, you'll find a memorial and a poem written for the ten fallen soldiers.

← Station

Town Centre →

WANTED
Dr Beeching

REWARD

Bere Ferrers

THE TAMAR TIMES 1917

TRAGEDY ON THE TRACKS

On this tragic day, a poem for the brave men who lost their lives:

R.I.P

Who shall sing the song of them,
The wonder and the strength of them,
The gaiety and tenderness they bore across the sea?
In every heart's the song of them,
The debt that England owes to them,
The chivalry and fearlessness
That strove and won her free.

Ah, I love the smell of Dock Dung in the morning – and daffodils too! Here we are in Bere Alston – and it's 1910! There's Mary waiting for us; she's a grower here in the valley.

The steep slopes of the valley catch the sun all day. For over 200 years they've produced daffodils, cherries, apples and all kinds of other soft fruit and flowers here. The soil was made even more fertile in the 1900s, with rubbish from Plymouth streets.

They called the mess of horse dung, fish guts, butchers' scraps and even human poo, Dock Dung. It was scraped up every morning and dumped in a huge smelly pile down at the Dockyard. Each day the Dock Dung was loaded onto big barges – 100 tons at a time – and floated down the River Tamar. Farmers and growers would wait at the quays to buy it, swearing that it was the best fertilizer they had ever used!

Mary's Story

I'm only seven, but I already help my parents with the picking on our farm. Four in the morning is time to get up. I pull on my clothes, grab my sclum and my dibber and set off for the hills. We make our sclums out of table forks, bending back the teeth and adding a long handle – they look like tiny rakes!

Sometimes 40 of us work together – we can pick a ton of strawberries in just one day. When I get older I'll learn how to grow 'double white daffodils'; you won't find them growing anywhere else in the world!

At the end of the day, we rush to get our fruit and flowers boxed and onto the train. Each pound of strawberries makes two shillings more at London's Covent Garden Market than at Devonport. The work may be hard, but my fingertips taste of strawberries, my hair smells of daffodils and I work in the sunshine all day long!

Mary

APPLES

Growers used to ship their crops by boat to Devonport Market. Then the railway opened, and trains from Bere Alston travelled to London and beyond. Growers could send fruit and flowers long distance, knowing they'd arrive, still fresh, in London's bustling markets, less than one day later!

By the 1950s nearly 10,000 people worked this land. Then railway branches closed and cheaper fruit and vegetables arrived from abroad. It became harder for the growers to make a living; hardly any of them are left today.

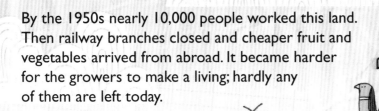

Bere Alston

WANTED
Dr Beeching
REWARD

DAFFODILS
STRAWBERRIES
PEARS

The Daily Tamar
1913
DOCK DUNG BANNED

"It's disgusting!" say the authorities. They've had too many complaints about the foul stench floating up from the Dock at Devonport, where Dock Dung is dumped ready to be transported to the fields by boat...

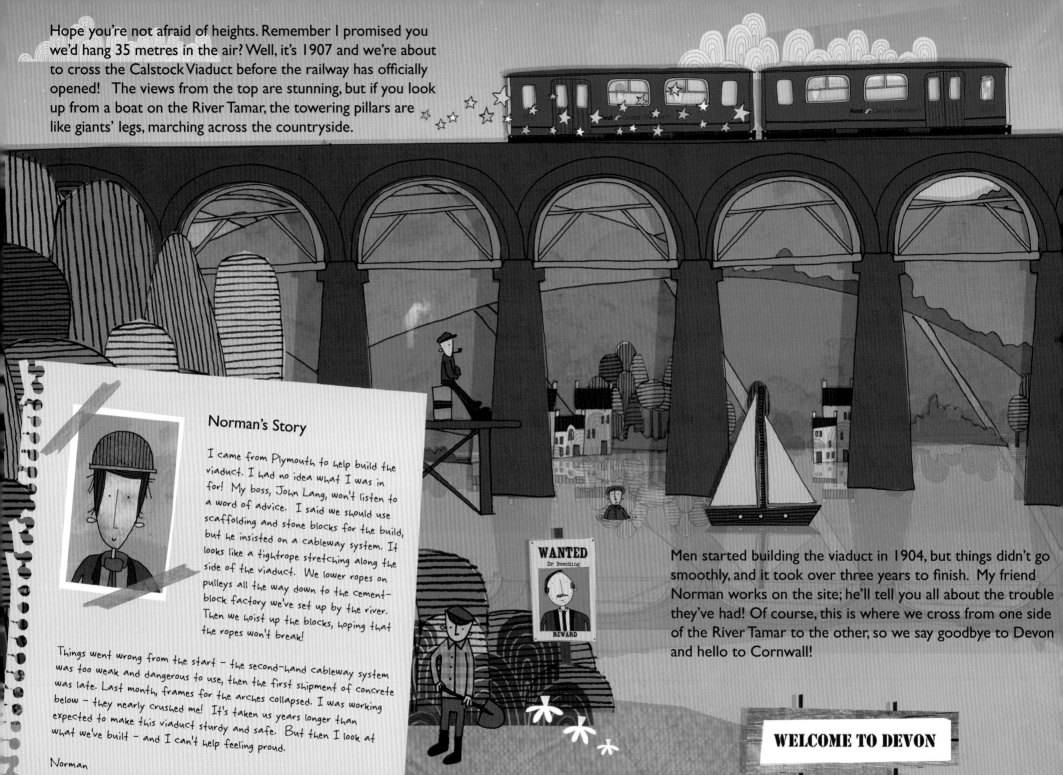

Hope you're not afraid of heights. Remember I promised you we'd hang 35 metres in the air? Well, it's 1907 and we're about to cross the Calstock Viaduct before the railway has officially opened! The views from the top are stunning, but if you look up from a boat on the River Tamar, the towering pillars are like giants' legs, marching across the countryside.

Norman's Story

I came from Plymouth to help build the viaduct. I had no idea what I was in for! My boss, John Lang, won't listen to a word of advice. I said we should use scaffolding and stone blocks for the build, but he insisted on a cableway system. It looks like a tightrope stretching along the side of the viaduct. We lower ropes on pulleys all the way down to the cement-block factory we've set up by the river. Then we hoist up the blocks, hoping that the ropes won't break!

Things went wrong from the start – the second-hand cableway system was too weak and dangerous to use, then the first shipment of concrete was late. Last month, frames for the arches collapsed. I was working below – they nearly crushed me! It's taken us years longer than expected to make this viaduct sturdy and safe. But then I look at what we've built – and I can't help feeling proud.

Norman

WANTED
Dr Beeching
REWARD

Men started building the viaduct in 1904, but things didn't go smoothly, and it took over three years to finish. My friend Norman works on the site; he'll tell you all about the trouble they've had! Of course, this is where we cross from one side of the River Tamar to the other, so we say goodbye to Devon and hello to Cornwall!

WELCOME TO DEVON

Somehow it seems right that we slowed down to 18.5 miles an hour after leaving Bere Alston – this section of the line is so steep and twisty, it's the slowest in the country. In 1907 people from Devon may not have minded the careful pace... folklore had it that the devil himself wouldn't go into Cornwall – for fear of being baked in a pasty!

WELCOME TO CORNWALL

THE TAMAR TIMES
EDGCUMBE ESCAPES

1483

Sir Richard Edgcumbe has escaped from his home, Cotehele House, chased by King Richard III's soldiers. He put a large stone in his hat and hurled it into the river. The soldiers heard a splash, saw his hat and assumed he had drowned himself.

Calstock in the 1850s wasn't the pretty little town we know today. In fact, hold your noses everyone – we're nearly there. With luck, my mate Percy will be waiting for us. He'll tell you all about life in this rough, smelly mining town. People have mined the valley since medieval times! Back then, the King gave boys two choices: work in the lead and silver mines, or join the military and fight to the death! Which would you choose?

The Daily Tamar

2007

GARDEN SWALLOWS WOMAN

A woman narrowly escaped with her life after being swallowed by her own garden when a 200-year-old mineshaft gave way beneath her.

This area is most famous for its copper mines. In the 1850s, Devon Great Consols was the richest copper mine in all of Europe. Then came the 1860s, when the price of copper dropped. Miners started to extract poisonous arsenic from the metal instead – it fetched a better price. At its peak, the Tamar Valley produced half of the whole world's arsenic. It's said that there was enough of the poison in the Cornish mines to kill every living creature on the planet. Yikes!

Percy's Story

Calstock's no place for the faint-hearted. No sewage system, no police, no manners — and that's how we like it! Most of the men here are miners. We work eight-hour shifts, with only short breaks to swig a drink and gobble down a pasty. And you'd better not be scared of the dark — the mineshafts are 250 metres deep! They're cold, damp and black as night.

In town it's so crowded that there aren't enough beds to go round. I work all night in the mine and in the morning I go home and wake up my mate for the daytime shift. Then I steal his bed and get some sleep. They may not be clean, but at least the beds in Calstock are never cold!

Percy

The Calstock Inn

As the price of arsenic fell too, the mines started to close. Miners left the valley to find work overseas. Now the mines are abandoned and crumbling, but you can still spot their tall chimneys sticking out of the ground as you travel down the line.

The hankies are out in Gunnislake today – we must be back in the early 1900s! During this time Gunnislake was as busy and bustling as Calstock. 'Gunnis' means 'mine working', but as the work declined, this station became known as 'the station of tearful goodbyes'...

TAMAR EXPRESS

WANTED
Dr Beeching
REWARD

The Daily Tamar
1912
MINERS SINK WITH TITANIC

Four Cornish miners have lost their lives on their journey to make a new start in America. Tragically, their vessel, the Titanic, sank after only four days at sea.

Many unemployed miners left from here by train to search out a living in faraway countries. Mining work was plentiful in South Africa, America, Australia and Mexico – but miners had to leave their families behind.

As trains pulled into the station, husbands, wives and children huddled together to say goodbye. Sometimes the miners were gone for a few months, sometimes years and sometimes they never returned.

Today, this is the last stop on the line, although it wasn't always...

In the 1960s, a man named Dr Beeching came along and changed Britain's railways for ever... Wait... who's that hiding behind his newspaper...? It's him – Dr Beeching! He's been on the train all along. You shouldn't be here, Beeching. This isn't your time. You're no friend to the railways and you're no friend of mine!

Gunnislake

Tom

Dr Beeching's Story

I was boss of British Railways in the 1960s. My report – the Beeching Report – called for one third of all British stations to close. I was asked to save money and that's exactly what I did. Gunnislake to Callington – CUT! Bere Alston to Okehampton and Lydford – CUT!

In all, I cut 5,000 miles of railway and the ungrateful people of Britain didn't stop complaining! Growers in the Tamar Valley whined that they couldn't get their fruit to the market any more... Commuters to the cities moaned that they had to move out of the countryside... Railway employees whinged when they lost their jobs... But I was only doing my job. Somehow the locals managed to save the line from Plymouth to Gunnislake, but if I'd had my way the entire line would have been closed down!

Dr Beeching

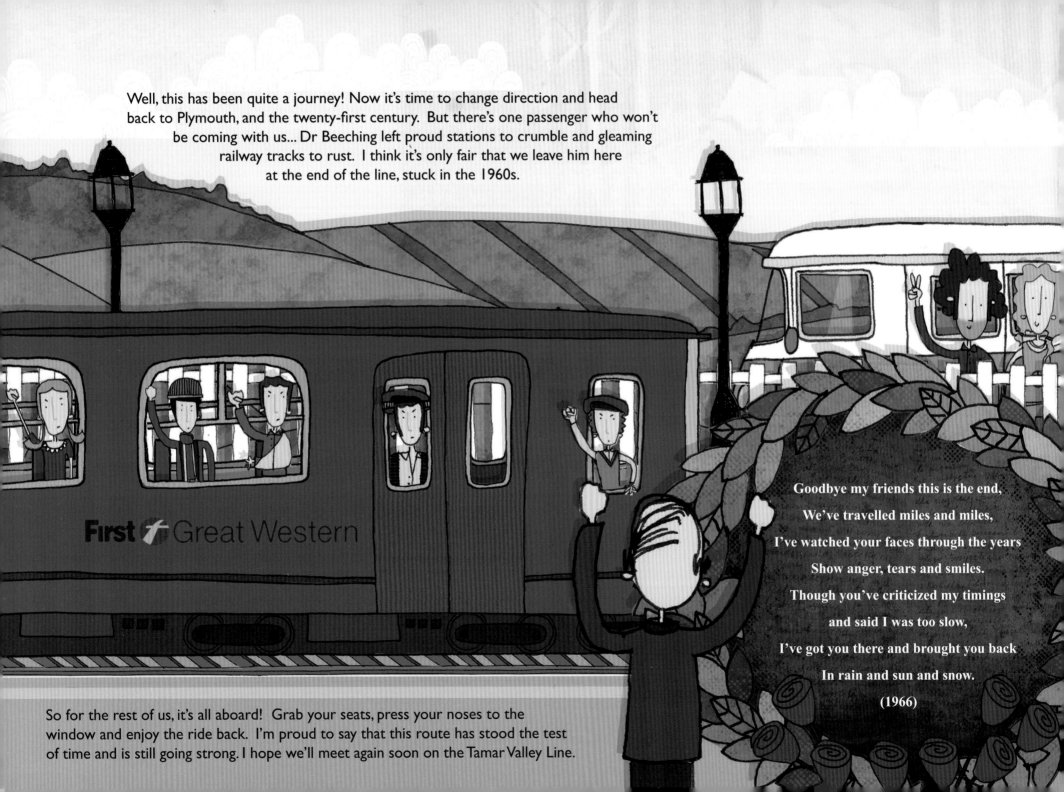

Well, this has been quite a journey! Now it's time to change direction and head back to Plymouth, and the twenty-first century. But there's one passenger who won't be coming with us... Dr Beeching left proud stations to crumble and gleaming railway tracks to rust. I think it's only fair that we leave him here at the end of the line, stuck in the 1960s.

First *f* Great Western

Goodbye my friends this is the end,
We've travelled miles and miles,
I've watched your faces through the years
Show anger, tears and smiles.
Though you've criticized my timings
and said I was too slow,
I've got you there and brought you back
In rain and sun and snow.

(1966)

So for the rest of us, it's all aboard! Grab your seats, press your noses to the window and enjoy the ride back. I'm proud to say that this route has stood the test of time and is still going strong. I hope we'll meet again soon on the Tamar Valley Line.